INI

GW00862887

INDUCTION

by Ruth Watts-Davies

The Industrial Society

First published 1973 by
The Industrial Society
Peter Runge House
3 Carlton House Terrace
London SW1Y 5DG
Telephone 071-839 4300

© *The Industrial Society, 1973, 1984, 1989*
Reprinted July 1990

ISBN 0 85290 448 7

Typeset by Barnes Design + Print Group, Maidenhead
Printed and bound in Great Britain by Belmont Press, Northampton

CONTENTS

FOREWORD

Whatever the discipline or level of management, the responsibilities of managers are many and various. It is their job to produce results with essentially just two resources—people and time.

To maximise the potential of both, most managers need some reminders and basic guidelines to help them.

The Notes for Managers series provides succinct yet comprehensive coverage of key management issues and skills. The short time it takes to read each title will pay dividends in terms of utilising one of those key resources—people.

Induction is one of the great neglected areas of management policy. Every year in Britain, hundreds of thousands of pounds are wasted on recruiting and training people who leave their jobs long before they have contributed their real potential to the organisation. Not all this wastage can be blamed on bad induction. But a great deal of it can, particularly in the case of young employees.

This booklet gives an outline of all the necessary questions to be addressed in the formulation of a good induction scheme, as well as providing a number of useful examples of procedures and activities.

ALISTAIR GRAHAM
Director, The Industrial Society

I

INDUCTION

INTRODUCTION

Recruitment and training are a major cost to any organisation. Employers therefore need to maximise staff retention to ensure that this investment is not wasted. The initial impression of an organisation on an employee usually stays with them, and it is therefore important to make this experience a positive one. Induction is a greatly neglected area of management policy which aims to achieve just this.

New members of staff need to have basic information about their terms and conditions of employment, trade union membership and their immediate working environment. However this is not enough. People, whatever their industry or profession, want to know how they fit into the organisation as a whole and how their work relates to that of other people and other departments. Naturally they also want to meet their colleagues and line managers.

All these things should be covered in an induction scheme. However, all too often there is no formalised system for ensuring that this takes place.

Recruits are left to 'pick things up as they go along' or taken on the traditional handshake tour. This is simply asking the new employee to adopt an indifferent attitude towards the organisation, thereby reducing the chances of that employee staying long enough to contribute their full potential. Labour turnover costs money too. In addition it reveals an unacceptable wastage of an organisation's human resources—the most valuable assets it has. Induction programmes assist in reducing labour turnover by integrating new employees effectively into the organisation.

The process of induction

Induction is the process by which new employees are integrated into an organisation so that they become productive as soon as possible.

In order to ensure that this happens quickly and effectively, the process needs to be planned, managed, and adopted into the organisation's overall training plans.

In order to arrive at an induction action plan there are three main questions to be considered.

1 What should we tell them?
2 Who should tell them?
3 When should they be told?

1

WHAT SHOULD
WE TELL THEM?

There are five main categories of information that should be given to new employees.

Organisational information

This should include information about the organisation including size, history, and if appropriate details of who the parent company is and/or its subsidiaries. It is important that employees know exactly who it is that they are working for.

Procedural information

This comprises information concerning organisational procedures which affect all members of staff. The information provided should include:

- terms and conditions of employment
- disciplinary and grievance procedures
- fire and bomb procedures
- standards or codes of dress
- rules on entering and leaving the premises.

Job information

This relates to what is necessary for a new employee to know in order to do a job effectively. The information provided should include:

- a job description detailing the major tasks and account-abilities of the job
- details of any training which is involved
- procedures for obtaining equipment, stationery, or tools
- a copy of relevant sections of an organisation chart as it is important to inform recruits not only of what they have to do but also why it is important and how it fits into the department and organisation.

Personal information

This is the area which affects a new employee's private life and personal needs, for example, how salaries are paid, where to eat, and the location of the toilet facilities. Everybody has anxieties on starting a new job and to have to ask about these fundamentals only adds additional stress.

Team information

Team information will provide knowledge of all those things which will encourage employees to integrate into the working group. This category needs to cover the informal as well as formal aspects of working life, e.g. the fact that 'we all go for a pint at lunch time on Fridays' can be more important to this process than knowing who the shop steward is.

2

WHO SHOULD TELL THEM?

The golden rule governing the passing on of information is that when in doubt, the informant should be the new employee's immediate line manager or supervisor. However, there are a number of people who could be involved.

The personnel department

The main role of the personnel department in induction is in devising and maintaining an effective system. Initial induction may be done in group sessions or individually, depending on the organisation. In either case personnel should be responsible for providing information on specialist areas such as contracts of employment, pension and sickness schemes, share option schemes etc. They can also be responsible for passing on organisational and procedural information.

The immediate boss

This is the person who has the greatest vested interest in an effective induction procedure and who is responsible for ensuring that the employee gets the right balance between job, personal, and group factors.

Induction also represents an ideal opportunity for boss and subordinate to get to know one another and to start developing their working relationship.

Responsibility for the induction of a new recruit should never be delegated. Other people in the department may become involved, but the immediate line manager should introduce them to the new employee and follow up to ensure that their work has been satisfactorily carried out.

On-job trainer

It can be of great benefit to give some responsibility for induction to one of the new employee's fellow workers. It can give the new recruit an opportunity to make a 'friend' which will be particularly helpful in the passing on of personal and group information. Every working group develops its own unwritten customs and habits and for someone to unwittingly contravene these customs can be both embarrassing and humiliating.

The shop steward/staff representative

New employees should be introduced to their shop steward or staff representative. As well as being able to provide information, these people are important in making sure that the new employee is aware of the channels of communication within an organisation.

A director or senior manager

A short interview with one of the new recruit's senior line managers will allow the recruit to recognise senior management and can give a wider appreciation of the role of the department. It also gives the manager an opportunity to meet every new recruit and to monitor the effectiveness of the induction programme.

3

WHEN SHOULD
THEY BE TOLD?

Induction is a continuing process and may well spread over several days or weeks after the recruit starts work. New employees are only able to take in a limited amount of information at any one time, and the aim of a systematic induction programme should be to cover all the ground in the shortest effective time.

Pre-employment

The induction process begins during recruitment and selection. Before joining an organisation, the new employee should be aware of the important terms and conditions of employment, and these should have been provided in writing. However, the recruit also needs to be given specific instructions for the starting day. These should include:

- where and when to report
- who to ask for
- what to bring
- where to park.

Employers should also prepare for the recruit's arrival by providing:

- all equipment, clothing, safety wear etc.
- a timetable for people who are involved in inducting the new employee.

Day one

Whatever the size of the organisation, what happens on the first day at work makes a big impression. Recruits should therefore be made to feel welcome by everybody that they meet. It is usual for new employees to report to the personnel department who will cover the essential paperwork with an employee either as part of a group induction or individually before taking them along to their department.

Once all the necessary paperwork has been completed — bank details, pension forms etc. — organisational and procedural information should be given. This should include disciplinary and grievance procedures.

New employees should be introduced to the people that they are going to work with so that there are some familiar faces in the department the next day. This should include the on-job trainer allocated to the recruit.

It is important to remember to restrict the information given on day one in order to maximise what is retained by the employee.

In the department

The aim of departmental induction is to ensure that new employees settle down into their work and that their levels of performance reach a set standard as soon as possible. The complexity and length of the departmental induction programme will vary according to the job.

Individuals should have their induction programmes detailed to them by their immediate line manager or supervisor. This means that they will understand what has been planned for them and will also allow them the opportunity to prepare questions in advance, minimising the tendency to only think of important things after the event.

The areas covered at this stage are job information and personal information. These can be given by the immediate line manager or supervisor and the on-job trainer. The extent of the role of the on-job trainer will be dependent on their skills and experience

Follow-up induction

After 8-12 weeks, the new employee should be settled into the organisation. Some will find this easier than others and some may develop problems which are potential reasons for leaving. All starters should therefore be followed-up individually and problems and concerns dealt with before they result in a possible resignation.

A formal follow-up induction also gives the opportunity to impart further information, e.g. education and training facilities or transfer policies, which it was not appropriate to cover in the initial induction period.

All new employees will have questions after this length of time and will probably want to know more about the organisation. It may therefore be appropriate to arrange a tour of another part of the company, e.g. Head Office or a staff visit to the factory.

4

SPECIAL CASES

While the principles outlined so far are the guidelines to good induction, there are some special cases. These require additional considerations over and above the normal induction process.

School leavers

Most school leavers will be nervous and excited about starting work and therefore need to be put at ease as soon as possible. They need to develop a positive attitude towards work and an effective induction programme provides an opportunity to ensure that any initial interest and enthusiasm which exists is developed and encouraged.

The induction programme for school leavers needs to place particular emphasis on ensuring that they appreciate their importance to the organisation and understand where their job fits into the greater whole.

In order to build commitment, there is a need to place considerable emphasis on why something should be done or done in a certain way, rather than just giving instructions. Opportunities for training and development should also be clearly outlined.

The use of an on-job trainer or 'mentor' can be of particular benefit to this category of new employee. A school leaver's confidence can easily be destroyed and such assistance will help ensure that they do not break any of the 'unwritten laws' of the workplace, as well as aiding the formal induction process.

Graduates

In graduate induction emphasis needs to be placed on giving an appreciation of how departments are inter-dependent. Technical graduates tend to see their own objectives simply in terms of their own subject and need to develop an appreciation of the constraints in which they will work. Management trainees need to understand the 'business'.

For this process to be fully effective, it is essential that a graduate's induction programme involves undertaking specific jobs or tasks at all stages. This will ensure that induction is perceived by the graduates as relevant. This helps to maintain their motivation and interest.

Women returning to work after a career break

Women returning to work have special anxieties. One of these may manifest itself as lack of confidence—feeling that they will not be able to cope because of the changes in working practices and technology.

An effective induction programme should recognise this and place particular emphasis on skills training. This will build confidence and enable the employee to feel that they can make a worthwhile and valued contribution to the organisation.

Minority groups

Induction programmes should take account of any special needs of minority groups. If language is a problem, training should be arranged in order to help the new employee integrate into the organisation.

5

HOW INDUCTION
IS CARRIED OUT

Whatever the size or resources of an organisation, induction should be:

- part of a systematic plan
- written down
- recorded at each stage as completed
- constantly monitored.

The best method of achieving this is to draw up a checklist of the items to be covered as shown in Appendix 1.

The basic principles of induction should always be the same. However, the specific way that a programme operates is dependent upon the individual organisation and the resources that it has available.

Large organisations

In large organisations with a personnel and training department, group inductions can be arranged. These can cover the organisational and procedural information categories. It is useful to use visual aids such as films and slides whenever possible, as what is seen makes more impact than what is heard.

Specialists should be used wherever possible to talk about their own subjects. These should include:

- The Personnel Officer (terms and conditions of employment)
- The Security Officer (security policies and procedures)

- The Health and Safety Officer (accident reporting and standards of health and safety).

A number of different speakers will break up the day, making it more interesting and therefore aid the retention of facts.

It is important to ensure that new employees are introduced to their line manager or supervisor at the end of the group induction day and are given clear instructions as to where to report the following day. They will then be ready for their departmental induction, which is when they will start to receive job information.

Small organisations

In smaller organisations with no personnel and training department, it is not possible to arrange group inductions. Induction programmes therefore need to be specifically tailored to each individual's needs from day one. The induction will be wholly the responsibility of the new employee's immediate line manager or supervisor. The same checklist for large organisations can be used, but the line manager or supervisor will have to decide who is best qualified within the organisation to cover the various items. This will then mean arranging meetings with specialist members of staff including:

- the person responsible for wages and salaries
- the union/staff representative
- managers/supervisors from other departments.

It is essential that everybody involved is fully aware of the programme and the role that they are expected to play in it.

II

APPENDICES

INDUCTION CHECKLIST

Name of employee .... Date of starting			

SUBJECT	RESPONSIBILITY	SIGNATURE (of employee)	DATE
1 ORGANISATIONAL INFORMATION			
a) Group Information Name History Products/services Locations	*e.g. Personnel Manager*		
b. Company Information Name Organisation Product/service Customers Managers' names			
c) Welfare and Benefits Canteen Lockers Medical Sports Social Share option			

(cont.)

2 PROCEDURAL INFORMATION

a) *Contract of employment*
Hoursof work
Notice periods
Wages/salary
  where/when/
  how
Bonus schemes
Pension scheme
Sickness
  notification
  certification
  pay
Holidays
Pay slip

b) *Rules and Procedures*
Company rules
  misconduct
  codes of dress
Disciplinary
Grievance
Appeals
Safety
  fire and bomb
  exits
  extinguishers
  First aid
  Accidents
  Safety reps

c) *Communications Procedures*
T.U. recognition
Staff council
Co. newspaper
Briefing groups

(cont.) **d) Manpower Development Policies** Day release Fees assistance Performance appraisal Promotion Transfer **3 DEPARTMENT INFORMATION** Organisation Names Rules Meal breaks Clocking in Clocking out Job description Equipment Standards of performance Hours			

2

GROUP INDUCTION TIMETABLE

9.00 a.m.	Welcome and Introduction	Personnel Mngr.
9.30 a.m.	Paperwork — Collection of P.45's Bank details	Wages Superv.
10.00 a.m.	Video History of the Organisation	Training Mngr.
10.30 a.m.	Coffee	
10.45 a.m.	Conditions of Employment	Personnel Mngr.
11.30 a.m.	Company Rules and Procedures	Personnel Mngr.
12.15 p.m.	Welcome from Managing Director	Managing Dir.
12.30 p.m.	Lunch	
1.30 p.m.	Welfare and Benefits	Personnel Mngr.
2.00 p.m.	Education and Training	Training Offic.
2.30 p.m.	Safety Procedures	Safety Officer
3.00 p.m.	Security Procedures	Security Offic.
3.15 p.m.	Tea	
3.30 p.m.	Issue Uniforms	Training Offic.
4.15 p.m.	Meet Department Heads	
5.00 p.m.	END	